Departure into Emptiness

AF284544

Jupp Hartmann

Departure into Emptiness

Climate Crisis, Idleness and Mysticism

Essay

© 2020 Jupp Hartmann

Produced and edited by:
Herstellung und Verlag:
BoD – Books on Demand,
Norderstedt, Germany

ISBN: 978-3-7519-6951-2

I took a walk in the woods,
So as to look for nothing.
(Johann Wolfgang von Goethe)

I.

Not as much! That is the imperative of our age: less plastic, less CO2, less consumption, less stress. That sounds like a renunciation: of meat, of flying, of driving cars.

But does this necessarily have to be a renunciation? It would be renunciation to deny yourself the fulfillment of a deep desire. Not doing something because there is a better choice: that is freedom.

There are good reasons to use that freedom: needing less can be full of its own pleasure. It means being less dependent and - instead of constantly chasing after the satisfaction of needs - having more time for the really important things.

"Those who have lost by being moderate are rare."
(Confucius, Analects, IV.23)

II.

Doing and leaving are what shape our perception of the world. A woodcutter, a biologist and an investor perceive the same forest in a completely different way. Whoever is taking on a task must be careful not to be taken over by the task. The more the focus is on predetermined goals, the more the view of collateral damage is lost.

In a world of numbers and financial streams, everything becomes a means to an end. The earth becomes a raw material warehouse and people become human capital. Everything becomes a utility. What is useless or not useful enough from an economic point of view is in danger. Primeval forests are being cut down; animal and plant species are becoming extinct; in the name of utility a huge destruction is underway.

It would often be better if less were done. But this is difficult to achieve, because many people despair when they have nothing to do. They cling to their occupations. Often work is the centre of their lives - and for many it is the source of their identity.

In our performance-oriented times, this can be seen with extreme clarity. That it is not a new phenomenon, however, is proven by a more than two thousand year old text from China:

"When the farmer has nothing more to do with grass and weeds, he has nothing more to hold on to; when the merchant has nothing more to do with alleys and markets, he has nothing more to hold on to. Only when the people of the crowd have their daily work, do they make an effort. The craftsmen

depend on the skill and handling of their tools to feel themselves. If he cannot accumulate money and goods, the scrooge becomes sad. If power and influence do not expand steadily, the ambitious man becomes desolate. The slaves of power and wealth are only happy when in the process of change. If they find a time when they can act, they cannot stop acting. They all follow their path with the same regularity as the cycle of the year. They are caught up in the world of things and cannot change. So they run along, internally and externally trapped, sinking into the world of things and never coming back to themselves. Oh, how sad!" (Zhuangzi,XXIV.4)

So what can be done is done - and that is often much more than what needs to be done. We virtually suffocate under the mass of products that our productivity produces.

III.

Idleness. A word that has fallen into disrepute. Idleness, as the proverb warns, is the root of all vice; and more than a few even see in it the worst of all vices: the refusal to perform in a performance-based society.

The calls for deceleration, which are becoming louder and louder, have rehabilitated idleness to a certain extent in recent years. In the wellness sector at least it has found a firm place - and in countless magazine articles when it has to do finding oneself or burnout syndrome.

Idleness requires free time. This is more than leisure time: it is a time free of constraints, empty time that can be filled with what the moment offers.

Caught in the daily hustle and bustle, it is difficult to develop new perspectives. One is so busy mopping up the water that one does not even think of turning off the tap.

In order to get a grip on things at any time, your hands should be free. Being idle means to have time to do the right thing at the right moment.

IV.

Inspiration. The Muses like idleness. To be kissed by the Muse is the pictorial description of what many artists experience: a higher power seems to guide the creative process. This process is more of a letting happen than a conscious creation. Not the conscious ego - *it* paints, *it* writes, *it* composes. This state is called Flow.

In this way, making art becomes a communication with something unknown. Are higher powers at work here? Or is it simply neurobiological processes? Either way, it seems like a miracle.

But the flow does not come on command. You can only create good conditions for it. There's an ancient Chinese story about that.

"A wood carver carved a bell stand. When the bell stand was finished, all the people who saw it were amazed at its divine work. The Prince of Lu also looked at it and asked the Master, 'What is your secret?' The latter replied, 'I am a craftsman and know no secrets, and yet there is one thing that matters. When I was about to make the bell stand, I was careful not to consume my life force in other thoughts. I fasted to bring my heart to rest. When I fasted for three days I no longer dared to think of reward and honour; after five days I no longer dared to think of praise and blame; after seven days I had forgotten my body and all my limbs. At that time I also no longer thought about the court of Your Highness. Thus I was collected in my art, and all infatuations of the outside world had disappeared. Afterwards I went into the forest and looked at the trees in their natural growth. When the right tree came before my eyes, the bell stand was ready in front of me, so that I only had to put my hand on it. If I had not found the tree, I would have given up. Because I let my nature interact with the nature

of the material, that's why people think it's a divine work.'" (Zhuangzi, XIX.10)

V.

Art is often the art of omission. Capturing the atmosphere of a place with just a few strokes of the pen or grabbing the audience with a few notes is considered high art. It is often important not to do too much. If you try to speak a text in a particularly beautiful way, you will quickly appear artificial. If at a jam session all the participants constantly wanted to show all their skills, it would be very exhausting to listen to. Only when others hold themselves back can individuals come to the fore with their solos.

As much as through the emphasis of its tones a rhythm gets its special character through its pauses. A scale gets its special sound by omitting certain semitone steps.

The white area left blank on an old Chinese ink painting appears like the water of a river or like wafts of mist between the mountains. The emptiness here is an essential element of the composition.

In the early twentieth century, abstract painting developed through an increasingly consistent omission of all references to objects from the outside world.

This led to an undreamt-of freedom in dealing with colours and forms. And since there is no predetermined meaning in abstract paintings, they are an invitation to the imagination to go walking.

VI.

Let it happen! Trust in the momentum of the creative process! That was my basic attitude for decades when I was artistically active. For me, abstract painting became a voyage of discovery. Painting always had a meditative aspect for me. When I painted, I let the spontaneous impulses of my body take their course; I let my hands do it, without a plan, without thinking. I tried to leave the door to chance as wide open as possible. What happened to me often went far beyond what I could have thought up by myself.

I playfully found my artistic way. Over the years I did a lot of different things: pictures made of ceramic tiles, lit objects, digital art, abstract animations ...[1]

It was not a planned development. One thing led to another, each connected to the other, appearing in retrospect to be logical. But for me, every new turn was a surprise. I saw my own artistic development in

---

[1]My art can be found online at www.jupphartmann.de and on Instagram at jupp.hartmann.art

the way that train passengers sitting with their backs to the direction of travel see a landscape. I never saw what would come next.

I learned to have faith in the continuing process. And that I would discover more in my journey I'd ever dreamed of.

VII.

Cognitive methods. The modern sciences are atheistic in their methods, i.e. the recourse to religious beliefs is taboo in the scientific framework for good reasons. This does not mean, however, that one needs an atheistic default position to do science. The atheism of science is purely methodical and not ideological. Even those who are scientifically active have questions that cannot be answered in this way. Then one can decide for or against believing something specific. As long as the scientific activity remains unaffected by this, all is well.

Besides, the sciences cannot prove an atheistic world view because their method is atheistic. They cannot prove what they presuppose. That would be a circular argument.

Just like a methodical atheism there is also a methodical spirituality. As an artist, I become more open to inspiration when I feel that there is something greater than my conscious self, and that I can open myself to this *something* in my creative process. I just need to have the capacity to be amazed. Miracles are more likely to happen when I beleave they are possible.

As little as scientific knowledge can support atheism, so can artistic experience serve as proof of a higher powers.

The word "inspire" comes from Latin and means "to breathe in". It raises the question: who is breathing in? But all answers to this question remain speculation.

It is possible, perhaps even reasonable, to talk about creative work with religious or esoteric vocabulary. Then one interprets experiences within a given pattern of explanation. This makes them easier to communicate. This is legitimate, but it proves nothing with regard to the pattern of interpretation.

Beyond all doubt, the experience itself remains: Intuition can flow more freely the less conscious control you exercise. It is an experience that probably all people can have, no matter what they believe or don't believe.

VIII.

Success. Basically, it's quite banal: of course my art will be better if I'm painting, focused on what I'm doing, and not constantly thinking about what others will say or whether my work will yield enough money. The freer my head is, the more attentive I can work. With attention comes wonder and with wonder comes awe. With awe I have a good chance of succeeding in what I do.

In his book *Effortless Mastery* the New York jazz musician Kenny Werner makes the observation *"(...) that there are good players who, for some reason, have little impact when they play. Everything works fine. They are 'swinging' and all that, but still, something is not landing in the heart of the audience." (p.10)* He attributes this to the fact that they are caught up in their thoughts and are far too much guided by ideas about how right it should be. *"One must practice surrendering control to a larger, or higher force. It's scary at first, but eventually liberating." (ibid)*

I very often experience my painting when others talk about their art, be it music, painting or literature. Whoever wants to taste abundance must become empty.

IX.

Emptiness is of crucial importance in Daoist philosophy:

"How *the nose breathes and the ear hears, is essentially emptiness. All things use what they don't have on the basis of what they have. If you don't believe this, just look at a flute or a pipe made of reeds.*" *(Huainanzi, XVI.6b)*

This is not about an abstract or metaphysical idea of emptiness, it is about the very concrete emptiness between things or within things. It's about emptiness interacting with what's there. An emptiness that can be experienced.

Emptiness means potential. An empty space can be filled, empty time can be used, an empty sheet can be used to write on.

Not burdening oneself with unnecessary things means freedom. To become empty in this sense is the best way to find oneself.

To be empty means to have room for abundance.

In "Huainanzi", a book written over 2000 years ago as a collection of knowledge for the Chinese emperor, it reads like this:

"A restless spirit does not feel well even on a nicely prepared bed with soft mats. Nor does it appreciate a meal of wild rice and juicy beef. Even sounding strings and flute tones do not give him any pleasure.

Only when the anger dissolves and the restlessness dies down does the food taste good. The bed becomes comfortable, the home safe and being on the road a pleasure.

From this point of view: our nature is open to joy, but it is also open to sorrow. Whoever struggles with things that do not give pleasure to his own nature and hinders what gives pleasure to it, will certainly become a sorrowful person, even if he possesses all the riches of the world and is revered as a son of heaven. In general, human nature loves peace and silence and not discord and noise. It loves rest and quiet and not trouble and toil. If the mind is permanently free of desire, it means peace. If the body is permanently free of tasks, it means rest. The one who allows his spirit to wander in peace and quiet, who allows his body to indulge in idleness, who simply waits for what heaven gives him, will find joy in his inner being and will be free from worries from the outside. Nothing can change his insight, be it as great as the whole world. Even if the sun and moon darken, nothing can stop him from his path. Even when he is low, he feels blessed, even when he has little, he feels rich." *(Huainanzi, XIV.59)*

X.

Desires tend to take over control. The ambitions of the ego endanger inner freedom. They lead to compulsive behavior and a limited view of things.

"Among the people of Chu was one who stole gold. Just when the market was at its busiest, he came, took it and left. When they detained him and asked, 'How can you steal gold in the middle of the market?' he only replied, 'I have seen no one. I only saw the gold.' When the mind deals with desires, it forgets what it is doing." (Huainanzi, XIII.10)

XI.

Overcoming the ego. Many religions and spiritual teachings demand this. Overcoming it sounds like a hard struggle, a heavy effort, an act of will, in short, a strong ego to tackle this task. How could the ego be overcome in this way?

Asceticism can become a trap. The ego indulges itself in the rigid self-control it can exercise. There must be other ways to deal with the ego. This was also thought about in ancient China:

"The scholars in these times of decay do not understand how to get to the origins of their spirit and return to their roots. Above all, they try to model and polish their nature, to refine or suppress their original reactions in order to meet the demands of their time. Therefore, when their eye desires something, they intervene with prohibitions; when their mind delights in something, they restrict it with rites. They run further and further in circles, prostrating themselves, while the meat goes bad and inedible and the wine sour and undrinkable. Outwardly they tame their bodies, inwardly they scourge their spirit. They destroy the harmony of Yin and Yang and inhibit the original way of their nature of responding appropriately to fate. This is why these people are full of worries throughout their lives. Those who follow the Dao are very different: they regulate the original responses of their nature, cultivate their consciousness, nourish it with harmony, and direct it appropriately. They enjoy the Dao and forget the low things; they rest in their potential and forget the trivial issues. Since their nature does not desire anything, they achieve whatever they desire. Since their mind does not seek pleasure, there is no pleasure they would not participate in. Those who stick to their natural answers preserve their potential. He who yields to his inner nature

preserves his harmony. Physically relaxed and unrestricted in their attention: such standards and regulations can serve as a model for the whole world."
(Huainanzi, VII.14)

XII.

Regulation instead of blocking. Not asceticism but self-cultivation is the path that the Huainanzi describes. To rest in one's own potential means knowing one's abilities, but not having to prove them all the time. This makes it possible to react appropriately in ever changing situations.

"Planning things in advance is not better than learning techniques. Acting is not better than having options for action. Intervening is not better than leaving things to the Dao. If you act on purpose, there are goals that you will not achieve. If you strive for things, there are things you don't attain. So human beings come to their limits while the Dao pervades everything." (Huainanzi, XIV.24)

This kind of restriction does not mean renunciation, but the greatest possible sovereignty. And on the way there, it is not the effort that counts, but finding balance and peace. The less willpower is needed for this, the better.

That is easier said than done. We are simultaneously sexual, social, intellectual and spiritual beings. Our actions are determined by very different impulses, which are often difficult to reconcile. What we call "I" is actually a bundle of conflicting interests:

- There are the biological factors. Part of our behavior is hormonal. That's in the interest of the survival of our species.
- In addition to the preservation of our species, we are naturally interested in the preservation of our own existence. We nourish ourselves and take care of our bodies.
- At the same time we are social beings. We are integrated into social structures in which we take on tasks and place ourselves in hierarchies and power structures or rebel against them.
- We also enter into closer relationships with individuals, such as love relationships and friendships. Here again, completely different qualities are required than those normally found in social life.
- Through our language we are also involved in all types of discourses and much talk. Our conceptual thinking influences our perception and our actions. We develop opinions and beliefs.

- But intellect alone is not enough for us. We exceed its limits when we trust our intuition or develop creative abilities.
- Spiritual longings also play a role. The desire to transcend individual life proves again and again to be a powerful driving force behind human action.

We must somehow bring these different layers together. If one of them is too dominant, there is a danger that it will disturb the others. Those who strive too much for power are more likely to have difficulty developing loving relationships. Those who focus too much on the intellect may lose touch with their own bodies, and overly testosterone-driven men run the risk of coming into conflict with the rules of society.

But also if one of these layers is permanently suppressed, the consequences can be disastrous. For example, rigid sexual morals can not only limit the ability of individuals to have relationships, they can also poison the social climate. Tyranny is often accompanied by hostility to pleasure. So is political or religious fanaticism.

What we are depends decisively on how we deal with the demands of the various layers and how we resolve conflicts between them.[2]

XIII.

What does "me" mean? What does "I want" mean? Do all the parts of my personality want that? I can identify with each one of them, so much that I largely forget the others. In a moment of sexual ecstasy my intellect pauses, but the next day, in a lively discussion, I perceive myself completely as an intellect.

To which of these parts do I attribute "I"? All together? Or to all, one after the other? Or to the consciousness that sometimes perceives the one, sometimes the other? But sometimes I am also asleep.

The more I try to find myself, the more I slip away. I find many things I can identify with, but they are all snapshots. I am actually only the empty stage on which all these things can take place. Sometimes I

---

[2]The seven levels described here derive from the seven chakras, the energy centers in the body that play a major role in the religious tradition of India. For the energy to flow freely in the body, the individual chakras must be in harmony with each other. This idea has a very practical use, regardless of its spiritual dimension. It makes it easier to keep track of the different aspects of life and not to neglect any of them.

think of myself as the director, but the performance doesn't go according to my instructions, even though I have my input in the whole thing. The atmosphere of the play can be very different depending on the stage.

XIV.

The goal of many spiritual practices is to become empty, according to widespread opinion. For many people this is not a pleasant idea. They associate it with apathy and dullness.

But I do not have to become empty. I am already empty anyway. I am merely the stage on which the drama of my life takes place. It is enough to realize this emptiness and make the best of it.

Emptiness attracts abundance, and so I have a natural part in the abundance of the world. The point is not to become empty, but to keep the stage ready - and to invite the right actors.

XV.

The great art of life is to harmonize as much as possible the different impulses that determine our lives. One possible way to achieve this is lifelong learning. This is what Confucius says when looking back on his life:

"At seventy, I was able to let my heart's impulses flow freely without transgressing the right measure." (Analects, IV.23)

So personal desires and external demands coincide, but only after a lifelong effort.

Confucian learning is something fundamentally different from learning in the modern sciences. It is not so much about constantly opening up new areas of knowledge and arriving at new insights. Rather, the old, proven things are to be learned. Through tireless practice, the desired skills will be deepened over time. Sequences of action that require full attention at the beginning become more and more automatic. They become part of the body's memory and can finally be executed without thinking about it.

This form of learning is still widespread in East Asia today. In China, Taiji chuan is practiced in many parks early in the morning and in the evening, often in larger groups. Newcomers imitate the more advanced ones. Usually, almost nothing is explained. It is not theoretical understanding that ultimately leads to an improvement in form, but frequent repetition.

XVI.

Return to nature! This is the Daoist alternative to the constant self-improvement according to the Confucian way.

"That oxen and horses have four legs, that is their heavenly nature. To restrain the horses' heads and pierce the oxen' noses, that is human influence. So it is said: He who does not destroy heavenly nature through human influence, who does not disturb his fate through conscious intentions, who does not damage his name for the sake of gain, who carefully preserves his own and does not lose it, returns to his true nature." (Zhuangzi, XVII.6)

In Chinese, nature means 自然 (zi ran), which means "by itself so" or "by itself right". According to this, nature is what is right by itself without human intervention. Through human action, nature is in danger of becoming unbalanced. Since we ourselves are also part of nature, we also endanger our own naturalness through our actions. The striving for power, fame and wealth destroys inner peace. But moral concepts and a sense of duty can also alienate us from our nature.

"Concepts are general tools; one should not put too much emphasis on them. Love and duty are emergency huts of the ancient kings. One can stay there

for a night, but not live there all the time. Other-
wise those who watch us will make too great de-
mands on us. The highest people of ancient times
used love as a path, and duty as a shelter to wander
in the open space of idleness. They nourished them-
selves from the field of desirelessness and stood in
the garden of needlessness. Walking in idleness is
non-action. Desirelessness is easy to feed, and need-
lessness requires no effort. The ancients called it:
wandering in which one plucks the truth. But those
who keep wealth for their lives are begrudging of
other people's income. Those who keep fame for
their lives are envious of the reputation of others.
Those who are devoted to power are not able to
grant influence to others. When they have these
goods in their hands they tremble, and when they
have to give them away they go into mourning, and
the One finds no room where it could be reflected.
When you consider their eternal restlessness, you
have to say that these are the people whom heaven
has condemned to slavery." (Zhuangzi, XIV. 5)

XVII.

Doing by not doing (wu wei) is the golden road
of Daoist philosophy. It doesn't mean doing nothing at all, it's more about doing things very
effectively. Those who reduce their needs to the
essentials have to act less. On the other hand, those

who are very ambitious run the risk of missing the essential. Inner conflicts are pre-programmed.

If someone goes to a party for fun and to make business contacts as well, two motivations run against each other and the result will hardly be satisfactory.

"Those who follow the path, their will is supple, but their actions are strong. Their mind is empty, but their reactions are precise. What we understand by supple will: pliable and tender, calm and quiet, hidden even when others do not dare to, acting when others are not able to, calm and carefree, acting without missing the right moment, whirling around with the ten thousand things without anticipating or initiating anything, simply responding appropriately to the issues." (Huainanzi, I.10)

XVIII.

Freedom is highly embattled. It is constantly threatened. Political freedom can only last if there are enough people who also want to be free. This requires a culture of freedom. The more you experience freedom, the more you learn to appreciate it.

People who suffer from burnout may have political freedom and freedom of contract, but they will hardly feel free. Those who are always under pressure of performance have difficulty finding themselves. Idle time is important in order to discover their own possibilities.

But idleness is also important in order to be able to participate in political events. Only those who have enough time can become active at the right moment. Already Aristotle knew that the power of despots is least endangered when everyone has to work to exhaustion. At a time when despots are becoming more numerous, it is therefore especially important to give more room to idleness.

XIX.

Boredom is the spectre that drives many to take refuge in permanent employment. But bridging boredom with distractions that gradually turn out to be just as boring only prolongs the boredom.

Boredom is a feeling of emptiness. There is nothing interesting here. Everything is boring. But where everything is dull and empty, there is room for creation.

Boredom is a yearning, a longing for something that makes time forget, a desire to experience wonderful things or do wonderful things. Friedrich

Nietzsche calls boredom "(…) *that unpleasant windless calm of the soul that precedes the happy journey and the merry winds." (The joyful Science, 1st book, 42nd chapter)*

Boredom is hard to bear. You have to learn to endure it. Zen practitioners who sit for hours in front of a white wall do it their way.

There is power in silence. But the way to tranquility is often through boredom.

Boredom changes the sense of time. A while stretches. I can linger long on something. My perception changes. Suddenly the world is timed differently. My thoughts change course. Other perspectives open up.

Flashes of inspiration arise in the tension between boredom and the will to do something.

XX.

Congestion is often the result of fleeing from boredom. Whether the stomach is overfilled or the brain with information, digestion is often difficult.

Nan'in, a Japanese Zen master during the Meiji era, once received a highly educated university professor who visited him to learn about Zen. Nan'in served tea. He poured the tea into his guest's cup until it was full, and continued pouring even after the tea had already flowed over the rim. The professor watched this abundance until he could no longer hold on to himself and shouted: "Enough, the cup is already overflowing!" - "Just like this cup," Nan'in said, "you are full of your own opinions and speculations. How can I show you Zen before you hand me an empty cup?" (According to Günter Wohlfart)

In a sermon of the Christian mystic Meister Eckhart (1260 - 1328) it says

"No vessel can contain two kinds of potion. If it is to contain wine, the water must be poured out inevitably; the vessel must become empty and bare. Therefore, if you are to receive divine joy and God, you must necessarily pour out the creatures. Saint Augustine says: "Pour out so that you may be filled. Learn not to love, that you may learn to love. Turn away, that you may be turned back. In short, everything that is to be receptive and absorbent should and must be empty." (German Sermons and Tracts, p.144)

According to the Islamic mystic Jalal od-Din Rumi (1207-1273)

"The wine of divine grace is boundless:
All limitation comes only from the imperfections of the cup.
The moonlight fills the sky completely from east to west;
How far it can fill your parlor depends on the windows.
Great honour is bestowed, my friend, upon the cup of your life:
Prince Love created it to contain His eternal wine."
(The teachings of Rumi, p.23)

XXI.

Mystical traditions of different cultures have always emphasized the importance of inner emptiness.

Emptiness creates space for new experiences. Emptiness opens up more room for imagination and intuition. These are very practical effects, useful for everyday life. But when mystics describe their experiences, there are completely different dimensions involved.

They talk about ecstasy, about the experience of God, about the knowledge of being one with all beings and with God. Of course, all this is no confirmation of any religious doctrine. The fact that someone believes he is communicating with higher powers is no proof of the existence of these powers. But obviously there is a lot going on in our brains when we reduce the external stimuli and the inner urge for activity.

The exuberant language with which mystical experiences are often described gives some idea of the intensity of these experiences. The journey into the inner emptiness is a journey into infinity. The inner cosmos is as incomprehensible and overwhelming as the outer cosmos. How one subsequently interprets the experiences of this journey strongly depends on the specific cultural means of expression.

Mystical experiences are not a privilege of any particular religion. Even those who do not believe can make them. They are not bound to any religion, but religions have a vocabulary that is particularly suitable to describe them. Mystical experiences are usually embedded in religious traditions, however they point beyond them.

Therefore, mystical thinking can build bridges between religions where fanaticism sees only abysses. The exchange of mystical experiences can facilitate dialogue between religions. Dogmas separate the religions, mystical experiences open ways to connect them.

Today we are in the favourable situation of having access to mystical texts from many different times and countries. Thus it is possible to see mystical experiences in a new light, to crystallize what they have in common and to relativize what is due to the respective spirit of the times and the cultural background.

In this essay I will mainly refer to Daoist writings. They are more philosophical than religious texts. Mystical experiences are treated without recourse to religious dogmas. This facilitates access for people who are not religious. But the experiences themselves are not Daoist, they are also found in Western mysticism. So for me the Chinese classics are also a key to the understanding of invaluable Western traditions, which have largely been forgotten by centuries of thoroughly justified criticisms of religion.

XXII.

Time currents drag people along with them. Even those who engage in the mystical journey inwards are not unaffected by political and religious debates. Mystical experiences do not make you infallible. So even mysticism is entangled in the course of things and never completely free from the dark sides of the respective culture.

In Christian mysticism, for example, the attempt to defeat the ego has repeatedly led to extremely body-hostile practices.

From the original Greek meaning of the word, an *ascetic* is actually someone who is dedicated to a cause, an athlete for example. The fact that in Christianity asceticism often turned into self-torture is certainly also rooted in the idea that after death the soul expects either paradise or eternal damnation including the tortures of hell. This creates fears, and fears favour rigid attitudes.

Zen Buddhism, which aims at a mystical experience of emptiness, strongly influenced the attitude of Japanese samurai who tried to leave their ego behind in favor of military discipline. The combination of mysticism and warriorism eventually led to the involvement of Zen followers in the war crimes of Japanese militarism during the Second World War.

Mystical immersion is about leaving the ego behind. But that cannot mean submitting to another ego. Leaving the ego behind means abandoning identifications, especially those with foreign goals. It means to become free from conditioning and compulsions and not to submit to a foreign authority.

Both goals could not be more different, but their path is partly the same, they lead through the recognition of the inner emptiness. So there is the danger that spiritual search might be instrumentalized for foreign purposes - even for military ones.

Those who seek guidance on the spiritual path quickly get into a guru dilemma. Teachers can be a great help, but they can also lead others completely astray.

Highwaymen prefer to prey on lucrative trails. On the way to enlightenment - or to paradise - there is much to be gained. Many are so focused on the promising goal that they do not pay attention to the path. There they are easy prey.

Religions can have a strong impact. That is precisely why rulers try to control them, and power-hungry people invoke them. The history of religions is impossible to comprehend without considering the history of their abuse. There are good reasons why many people reject religions. Power interests have generated much fanaticism and dogmatic paralysis.

But on the other hand, mystics have used language and images of religions to communicate their experiences. They were able to do so because religions themselves go back to such experiences.

XXIII.

The attempt to communicate the unspeakable
characterizes mystical texts. This has its pitfalls.

Our language is better suited to describe our everyday world than to pass on transcendental experiences. Language works because we are more or less familiar with what we are talking about. Everyone knows from personal experience what is meant when we talk about a tree. But the more something eludes our perception, the less our respective ideas about it coincide. How should we speak clearly and unambiguously about spiritual things.

Terms make things manageable. By naming things, we try to bring them under our mental control. Thus, talking about religion carries with it the danger of appropriation.

Religions have always been used for foreign purposes, but the attempts to protect them from this are just as old. Thus one of the Ten Commandments demands:

"Thou shalt not take the name of the Lord thy God in vain: for the Lord will not leave unpunished him that taketh his name in vain." (Moses, 2.20)

Another commandment demands:

"Thou shalt not make unto thee any graven image of God, nor any representation of any thing in heaven above, on the earth beneath, or in the waters under the earth." (ibid.)

The meaning of this commandment arises from the fact that all descriptions of God are only human projections and are based on human interests. Men create their gods according to their own image.

In the 6th century, Dionysius Areopagita formulated the outlines of a Negative Theology, which had a significant influence on the Christian mysticism of the Middle Ages. According to this, nothing can be said about God. He eludes conceptual understanding. One can only say that God is not what people attribute to him.

On the Internet I discovered a caricature: two pictures next to each other, posted by a dyed-in-the-wool atheist. Above one is written "The idea of God", above the other "The reality of God". "The idea of God" shows a magician with a magic wand, "The reality of God" shows a black surface. Nothing. Emptiness. What was meant as mockery from an atheist's perspective is for me a beautiful visual representation of what negative theology means.

"The Way that can be shown,
is not the eternal Way

The Name that can be named,
is not the eternal Name."
(Laozi, Daodejing, I.)

XXIV.

What language cannot capture, is easier to experience without language. In his book " The Spirit of Zen" Allen Watts describes the sermon of a Zen master:

"One day a master had just taken his seat when outside a bird began to sing. The master said nothing and everyone listened to the bird. When the song stopped, the master simply announced that the sermon had been preached and went away." (p.98f)

The joys of life are often found in the seemingly small things. The song of a blackbird can be moving. A squirrel scurrying past the balcony can evoke feelings of happiness, if I am receptive to it and not thinking about my next tax declaration.

When I have the idle time to get involved in the things that happen to me, I discover miracles everywhere. If you never forget how to be amazed, you will always fall in love with the beauty of nature. That is the best motivation to protect it.

XXV.

The climate crisis urges us to question the orientation towards materialism. Inner wealth is worth more than outer wealth. Consumption offers fewer moments of happiness than time spent in idleness. We could live much better and at the same time cause much less damage to our environment.

This requires a cultural change. A departure from performance pressure, competition and growth-mania. A political change would be the result. Other forms of economic activity would come into being as well. Quality instead of quantity.

If we want to change culture, it must be a joyful affair. Our time demands some sort of mystical hedonism.

"Have you ever heard that someone has done something extraordinary in a field he doesn't enjoy?" (Huainanzi, X.81)

Joy of life! Joy in the world! We must learn to love the world around us. Or to say it with the Beatles: *"All you need is love."*

"Love, love, love!"

XXVI.

All things are destined to perish. When we love, we are confronted with the fact that what we love is doomed. To develop a deep love for this world is on the one hand a way to greater joy of life. But it also makes us more vulnerable. There is no lasting joy without sorrow and grief. People we love die; projects we are enthusiastic about fail; and the more global our love becomes, the more global developments touch us: refugees drowning in the Mediterranean, climate change, species extinction.

It is in our very own interest not to simply accept these things, because that would mean becoming dull and thus also losing a large part of our capacity for happiness. Grief is the shadow of our joy. It is impossible to disconnect the two.

Everything that is, at some point, perishes, even that which we fight for with all our passion. Lasting success is not possible in this way. The traces we leave behind will be erased sooner or later. The baroque poet Andreas Gryphius describes it in a poem like this:

"You see wherever you look nothing but vanity on earth.
What the one is building today, the other will tear down tomorrow:

Where cities are standing now, there will be a meadow once,
On which a shepherd's child will be playing with the flocks."
(Andreas Gryphius, It's All Vain)

Everything that is made up of matter dissolves again sooner or later. That is the basic feature of all material things. But there is also an everlasting creative force which, despite the constant decay, always generates new wonders.[3] We human beings are part of this divine power which emanates from our deepest inner being. Creation is not something completed. It is what happens in every moment, also through our participation.

XXVII

Participation in the work of creation does not require excessive activity. It is enough to become receptive to the wonders of the world and to carefully partake in them.

To act in harmony with nature. Being nature. To bring forth good and beautiful things when the time is ripe and to rest when you see that it is good.

---

[3] Plotinus' philosophy in particular is centred around this theme.

Having time for what needs to be done. This requires a certain amount of idleness.

By the way, from its origin the German word *"Muße"* (idleness) is related to *"müssen"* (must). In order to do what needs to be done, you must have enough time. It is sometimes better if your day planner is empty. Emptiness creates freedom of movement.

XXVIII

"Thirty spokes meet in the wheel hub.
Its emptiness makes the wheel usable.
You form clay to create a vessel.
Its emptiness makes the vessel useful."
(Laozi, Daodejing, XI.)

It is the emptiness within us that allows us to draw from the full.

Sources

- Aristoteles: Politik. Translated by Franz F. Schwarz, Stuttgart, 1989
- Goethe, Johann Wolfgang: www.volksliederarchiv.de/ich-ging-im-walde-so-fuer-mich-hin/
- Gryphius, Andreas: Es ist alles eitel. www.deutschelyrik.de/es-ist-alles-eitel.302.html
- Huainanzi: Own translation, based on the ranslation by Mayor, Queen, Meyer, Roth, Puett und Murray (The Huainanzi, New York, 2010)
- Konfuzius: Gespräche. In: Die Lehren des Konfuzius. Translated by Richard Wilhelm, Frankfurt (Main), 2008
- Laozi: Daodejing. Own translation.
- Mose, 2. 20: de.wikipedia.org/wiki/Zehn_Gebote
- Meister Eckhart: In: Quint, Josef: Meister Eckehart, Deutsche Predigten und Traktate. München, 1963
- Nietzsche, Friedrich: Die fröhliche Wissenschaft. Leipzig, 1990 ,
- Rumi, Jalal od-Din: In: Andrew Harvey: Die Lehren des Rumi. München, 2001
- Watts, Alan: The Spirit of Zen, London, 1936
- Werner, Kenny: Effortless Mastery. New Albany, 1996
- Wohlfart, Günter: Zhuangzi (Dschuang Dsi) – Meister der Spiritualität. Freiburg im Breisgau, 2001
- Zhuangzi: Translated by Richard Wilhelm (Dschuang Dsï: Das wahre Buch vom südlichen Blütenland. München, 2004)

Cover photo: Martina Bölck: Gate at Mount Tai, China
Other pictures: Own works

Proof reading: Fergus Kelleher